HOW TO TAP A Maple!

by Stephanie Mulligan

Illustrated by Connie Rand

McSea Books

To Grampy, Grammie, Papa Bill & Grandma Pat—
For your endless love and support.

SM

To my husband, Lee, who loves me with all his heart, and lets my creative spirit flourish.

CR

Manufactured by Regent Publishing Services Ltd Printed November 2022 in ShenZhen, China

Hardcover ISBN: 978-1-7323020-8-2
Ebook ISBN: 978-1-7323020-9-9

Library of Congress Control Number: 2020923521

www.McSeaBooks.com

Publisher's Cataloging-in-Publication Data
provided by Five Rainbows Cataloging Services

Names: Mulligan, Stephanie, author. | Rand, Connie, illustrator.
Title: How to tap a maple! / Stephanie Mulligan ; Connie Rand, illustrator.
Description: Lincoln, ME : McSea Books, 2021. | Summary: Learn how maple syrup is made and where it comes from.
Identifiers: ISBN 978-1-7323020-8-2 (hardcover) | ISBN 978-1-7323020-9-9 (ebook)
Subjects: LCSH: Maple syrup--Juvenile literature. | Maple--Juvenile literature. | Illustrated works. | CYAC: Maple syrup. | Maple. | BISAC: JUVENILE NONFICTION / Science & Nature / Trees & Forests. | JUVENILE NONFICTION / Lifestyles / Country Life.
Classification: LCC TP395 .M85 2021 (print) | LCC TP395 (ebook) | DDC 641.3/364--dc23.

How to Tap a Maple!

Luke and Layla's winter was beginning to seem long
till Grampy started whistling his maple syrup song.

"It's time to teach you all about tapping maple trees.
So much to learn, and we'll have fun.
Pay close attention, please!"

When temperatures are perfect,
the sap will surely flow,

with daytime in the forties
and nighttime well below.

"Let's drill those holes," says Grampy. "We'll bore two inches in. Soon buckets will start filling, and collecting will begin.

The bigger, thicker maple trees can take more holes for sap. If one is big enough around, we'll grab another tap.

The spiles—or taps—are nice and clean. Make sure the fit is snug.
In two days, when we all come back, we'll find there's sap to lug."

Two days go by—the kids are here and eager to learn more.
They hope there's lots of sap to make maple syrup galore!

Grampy says, "You'll like this next part—lifting all the lids
and emptying the buckets will be exciting for you, kids!"

"Wow! There's so much sap in here! Just look at this one, guys."
Luke points to one nearby and says, "You won't believe your eyes!"

Luke dips his finger in the bucket for a drop to taste,
but this sap isn't very sweet. "Oh no, what a waste!"

"Don't worry, Luke. It will be sweet—I promise you it will.
First the sap will need to boil, then soon you'll get your fill."

Layla finds an empty bucket.
"Could this tree be dead?
Where's all the sap?" says Layla.
"Did we tap an oak instead?"

Luke and Grampy think that's funny.
They both laugh out loud.
It seems as though an oak tree
snuck into the maple crowd.

"Let's pour this sap into the pan and grab some logs of wood.
I'll light the fire," Grampy says, "so stand back where you should."

The evaporator's going. What a happy, sappy day!
As sugar bubbles in the pan the water goes away.

Layla glances past the door and spots a fox outside.
"It has pretty orange fur!" she says with eyes so wide.

Luke wanders out and hopes that he might see a moose or deer. What fun to see which animals are out this time of year.

Turning his head toward some rustling,
he says, "Hey, look over there.
Beneath that bush and to the left,
there's a little snowshoe hare."

"Listen hard," says Grampy,
"and you'll hear the Maine state bird.
That's the *chicka-dee-dee-dee*.
What a lovely song we've heard."

They hear the crackling fire—
the steam smells rich and sweet.
The children are excited
for this fresh, delicious treat.

The sap from trees was clear, but now it's thick and amber brown.
"It's nearly done," says Grampy. "It'll taste good goin' down!"

The sugar sand that formed before must now be filtered out.
Hot syrup runs into a pan beneath the draw-off spout.

Grampy takes his finishing pan to a small stove nearby.
"It needs to boil a little more, and you'll get some to try."

Finally, he fills his test cup with syrup from the pan.
He puts in his hydrometer. "Now read that if you can."

"I see some lines," says Luke, "and there's something about Brix."
Grampy says, "Look here, it's done! It floats at sixty-six."

He pours it through a cone-shaped filter into a pot below.
They load the syrup on the sled and homeward bound they go!

Counting all the trees they've tapped—there are one hundred thirty-three.
Ten gallons of sap per maple means a quart of syrup per tree!

Grampy says, "The syrup won't spoil if it's bottled hot."
The jars heat in the oven and the syrup in the pot.

"Let me hold the hot jars, Luke, and you'll take charge of the spout."
Layla watches them fill the jars as liquid gold flows out.

The cast iron pan is sizzling
with breakfast foods for dinner.
Pancakes, eggs, and bacon—served
with *SYRUP*. It's a winner!

At last, Luke and Layla try what they've been waiting for.
Their taste buds dance around and shout,

"*MORE! MORE! MORE!*"

"Oh, yum!" says Layla. "It's so sweet! Can I please have the rest?"
Then Luke replies, "Save some for me! This syrup is the best!"

Grampy serves a yummy feast. "It's time to eat!" they cheer.
Luke says, "Thank you, Grampy. We can't wait to help next year!"

Sugar Slang

Boiling: When the maple sap is hot enough to make the transition to maple syrup, the sap boils at 219° Fahrenheit.

Brix: A scale used to determine the amount of sugar in the maple syrup. This is important because in some locations the law states that maple syrup must have a density of at least 66% sugar to be sold.

Evaporator: A system that uses heat to boil sap, in order to make maple syrup. Water evaporates and turns into steam while the sugar stays and makes the syrup sweet.

Filter: A material used to remove any extra minerals or debris from the maple syrup.

Finishing Pan: The last pan used to boil the maple sap before it finally becomes maple syrup.

Firebox: The part of an evaporator that keeps the fire going and heats up the evaporating pan.

Grades: The grade of maple syrup can be detected by color, clarity, density, and taste. There are four grades of maple syrup, according to the international standards: Golden Color with Delicate Flavor, Amber Color with Rich Flavor, Dark Color with Robust Flavor, and Very Dark Color with Strong Flavor.

Hydrometer: A tool or instrument used to measure the density of maple syrup to detect how much sugar is present in the liquid.

40:1

Ratio: The ratio for maple syrup is about 40:1. This means it takes about 40 gallons of sap from a sugar maple tree to make 1 gallon of maple syrup.

Spile: A small metal or wooden spout used to draw sap from a maple tree.

Sugar House (also known as a sugar shack or sap house): A building or cabin where the process of turning maple sap into maple syrup takes place.

Sugar Sand: Gritty sediment that can be found in maple sap, once the sap boils. Before the maple syrup goes into a finishing pan, the sugar sand must be filtered out.

About maple tree species

Any maple species can be used to produce maple syrup, but sugar maple and red maple are best.

Maples are also used as firewood, and some species occasionally develop curly or tiger grain patterns which are especially valued for woodworking.

Some maple species have medicinal properties that were used by Native Americans. European pioneers even made ink from red maple bark.

Many maples are grown as shade and ornamental trees, including Bonsai trees.

Norway maple
Acer platanoides
65-100 feet
Uses: shade
tree, furniture,
woodworking

Sugar maple
Acer saccharum
80-110 feet
Uses: maple syrup,
furniture, woodworking

Red maple
Acer rubrum
50 feet
Uses: maple syrup,
furniture, woodworking

Silver maple
Acer saccharinum
80 feet
Uses: shade tree

Boxelder
Acer negundo
80 feet
Uses: shade tree,
woodworking

Mountain maple
Acer spicatum
10-30 feet
Uses: Tannins in the bark
can be used to tan leather.

Striped maple (moosewood)
Acer pensyvanicum
20-30 feet
Uses: Moose, deer, beavers,
and rabbits eat the bark.

About the Author

Stephanie Mulligan grew up in a beautiful village in western Maine and graduated from the University of Maine at Orono with her B.S. in Elementary Education and a concentration in English. She founded the publishing company McSea Books after teaching middle school. She is also the author of *How to Catch a Keeper*. Stephanie lives in Maine with her husband and their darling children. Find out more at stephmulligan.com.

© Photo by Tracie Murchison

About the Illustrator

© Photo by Lee Rand

Connie Rand, a native of Lincoln, Maine, graduated in 1969 from Portland School of Fine and Applied Art, now Maine College of Art, in Portland, from which she received an honorary Bachelor of Fine Arts in 2000. Her drawings and paintings are owned by collectors all over the United States and Canada. Connie illustrates *Quilter's World* magazine and other quilting publications for Annie's Publishing in Berne, Indiana. She and her husband Lee own Rand Advertising in Lincoln. They also own and maintain www.WelcomeToLincolnMaine.com, a website showcasing the Lincoln area, where they live with their three cats Ebenezer Scrooge, Marley, and Tiny Tim. To find out more visit connierand.com.